A Tradecraft Primer:
Structured Analytic Techniques
for Improving Intelligence Analysis

Prepared by the US Government

March 2009

This primer highlights structured analytic techniques—some widely used in the private sector and academia, some unique to the intelligence profession. It is not a comprehensive overview of how intelligence officers conduct analysis. Rather, the primer highlights how structured analytic techniques can help one challenge judgments, identify mental mindsets, stimulate creativity, and manage uncertainty. In short, incorporating regular use of techniques such as these can enable one to structure thinking for wrestling with difficult questions.

TABLE OF CONTENTS

THE "MIND-SET" CHALLENGE

Using the analytic techniques contained in this primer will assist analysts in dealing with the perennial problems of intelligence: the complexity of international developments, incomplete and ambiguous information, and the inherent limitations of the human mind. Understanding the intentions and capabilities of adversaries and other foreign actors is challenging, especially when either or both are concealed. Moreover, transnational threats today pose even greater complexity, in that they involve multiple actors—including nonstate entities—that can adapt and transform themselves faster than those who seek to monitor and contain them. Finally, globalization has increased the diversity of outcomes when complex, interactive systems such as financial flows, regional economies or the international system as a whole are in flux.[2]

The first hurdle for analysts is identifying the relevant and diagnostic information from the increasing volume of ambiguous and contradictory data that is acquired through open source and clandestine means. Analysts must also pierce the shroud of secrecy—and sometimes deception—that state and nonstate actors use to mislead. A systematic approach that considers a range of alternative explanations and outcomes offers one way to ensure that analysts do not dismiss potentially relevant hypotheses and supporting information resulting in missed opportunities to warn.

Cognitive and perceptual biases in human perception and judgment are another important reason for analysts to consider alternatives. As Richards Heuer and others have argued, all individuals assimilate and evaluate information through the medium of "mental models" (sometimes also called "frames" or "mind-sets"). These are experience-based constructs of assumptions and expectations both about the world in general and more specific domains. These constructs strongly influence what information analysts will accept—that is, data that are in accordance with analysts' unconscious mental models are more likely to be perceived and remembered than information that is at odds with them.

Mental models are critical to allowing individuals to process what otherwise would be an incomprehensible volume of information. Yet, they can cause analysts to overlook, reject, or forget important incoming or missing information that is not in accord with their assumptions and expectations. Seasoned analysts may be more susceptible to these mind-set problems as a result of their expertise and past success in using time-tested mental models. The key risks of mind-sets are that: analysts perceive what they expect to perceive; once formed, they are resistant to change; new information is assimilated, sometimes erroneously, into existing mental models; and conflicting information is often dismissed or ignored.

‪❝ Intelligence analysts should be self-conscious about their reasoning processes. They should think about how they make judgments and reach conclusions, not just about the judgments and conclusions themselves. ❞

—Richards Heuer,
The Psychology of Intelligence Analysis [1]

---

[1] Richards J. Heuer, Jr., *The Psychology of Intelligence Analysis* (Washington: Center for the Study of Intelligence, 1999).

[2] These observations were drawn from a lengthier treatment of cognitive bias found in the Sherman Kent Center's Occasional Paper, *Making Sense of Transnational Threats*, Vol. 3, No. 1, October 2004.

Common Perceptual and Cognitive Biases

Perceptual Biases

Expectations. We tend to perceive what we expect to perceive. More (unambiguous) information is needed to recognize an unexpected phenomenon.

Resistance. Perceptions resist change even in the face of new evidence.

Ambiguities. Initial exposure to ambiguous or blurred stimuli interferes with accurate perception, even after more and better information becomes available.

Biases in Evaluating Evidence

Consistency. Conclusions drawn from a small body of consistent data engender more confidence than ones drawn from a larger body of less consistent data.

Missing Information. It is difficult to judge well the potential impact of missing evidence, even if the information gap is known.

Discredited Evidence. Even though evidence supporting a perception may be proved wrong, the perception may not quickly change.

Biases in Estimating Probabilities

Availability. Probability estimates are influenced by how easily one can imagine an event or recall similar instances.

Anchoring. Probability estimates are adjusted only incrementally in response to new information or further analysis.

Overconfidence. In translating feelings of certainty into a probability estimate, people are often overconfident, especially if they have considerable expertise.

Biases in Perceiving Causality

Rationality. Events are seen as part of an orderly, causal pattern. Randomness, accident and error tend to be rejected as explanations for observed events. For example, the extent to which other people or countries pursue a coherent, rational, goal-maximizing policy is overestimated.

Attribution. Behavior of others is attributed to some fixed nature of the person or country, while our own behavior is attributed to the situation in which we find ourselves.

Intelligence analysts must actively review the accuracy of their mind-sets by applying structured analytic techniques that will make those mental models more explicit and expose their key assumptions. The techniques found in this primer are designed to assist in this regard by:

- Instilling more structure into the intelligence analysis.

- Making analytic arguments more transparent by articulating them and challenging key assumptions.

- Stimulating more creative, "out-of-the-box" thinking and examining alternative outcomes, even those with low probability, to see if available data might support these outcomes.

- Identifying indicators of change (or signposts) that can reduce the chances of surprise.

Incorporating findings derived from these techniques into our intelligence products also serves the policymaker by:

- Highlighting potential changes that would alter key assessments or predictions.

- Identifying key assumptions, uncertainties, intelligence gaps and disagreements that might illuminate risks and costs associated with policy choices.

- Exploring alternative outcomes for which policy actions might be necessary.

Strategic Assumptions That Were Not Challenged

1941 World War II

Japan would avoid all-out war because it recognized US military superiority.

Given that US superiority would only increase, Japan might view a first strike as the only way to knock America out of the war.

1950s Korean War

China would not cross the Yalu River in support of the North Korean government.

Red China could make good on its threats to counter "US aggression" against the North.

1962 Cuban Missile Crisis

The Soviet Union would not introduce offensive nuclear weapons into Cuba.

The Kremlin could miscalculate and believe it could create a fait accompli that a young US President would not be prepared to reverse.

1973 Yom Kippur War

Arabs knew they could not win because they had failed to cooperate in the past and still lacked sufficient air defenses to counter Israeli airpower.

A surprise Arab attack, even if repelled, could wound Israel psychologically and prompt international calls for cease-fires and diplomatic negotiations.

1989 German Unification

East Germany could not unify with the West Germany against the wishes of the Soviet Union.

The Soviet Union—under Gorbachev—might not be prepared to intervene militarily in Eastern Europe as it had in the past.

1998 Indian Nuclear Test

Conducting a nuclear test risked international condemnation and US sanctions and would threaten a newly elected coalition government.

A successful and surprise nuclear test could boost Indian nationalist pride and solidify public support for a shaky coalition government.

2003 Iraq's WMD Programs

Saddam failed to cooperate with UN inspectors because he was continuing to develop weapons of mass destruction.

If Iraqi authorities had destroyed their WMD stocks and abandoned their programs, they might refuse to fully acknowledge this to the UN to maintain Iraq's regional status, deterrence, and internal regime stability.

The analytic techniques in this primer are designed to help individual analysts, as well as teams, explore and challenge their analytical arguments and mind-sets. Some techniques are fairly simple to understand and employ—such as Brainstorming and Devil's Advocacy. Others are more complex and demand a greater degree of analytical sophistication, resource commitment, and time. All the techniques are included because they have helped other analysts avoid rigid ways of thinking or assisted them in exploring new outcomes or implications of an intelligence problem.

The techniques are grouped by their purpose: diagnostic techniques are primarily aimed at making analytic arguments, assumptions, or intelligence gaps more transparent; contrarian techniques explicitly challenge current thinking; and imaginative thinking techniques aim at developing new insights, different perspectives and/or develop alternative outcomes. In fact, many of the techniques will do some combination of these functions. However, analysts will want to select the tool that best accomplishes the specific task they set out for themselves. Although application of these techniques alone is no guarantee of analytic precision or accuracy of judgments, it does improve the sophistication and credibility of intelligence assessments as well as their usefulness to policymakers. As Richards Heuer notes in his own work on cognitive bias, "analysis can be improved."[3]

---

[3] Heuer, *Psychology of Intelligence Analysis*, p. 184.

KEY ASSUMPTIONS CHECK

List and review the key working assumptions on which fundamental judgments rest.

WHEN TO USE

A Key Assumptions Check is most useful at the beginning of an analytic project. An individual analyst or a team can spend an hour or two articulating and reviewing the key assumptions. Rechecking assumptions also can be valuable at any time prior to finalizing judgments, to insure that the assessment does not rest on flawed premises. Identifying hidden assumptions can be one of the most difficult challenges an analyst faces, as they are ideas held—often unconsciously—to be true and, therefore, are seldom examined and almost never challenged.

A key assumption is any hypothesis that analysts have accepted to be true and which forms the basis of the assessment. For example, military analysis may focus exclusively on analyzing key technical and military variables (sometimes called factors) of a military force and "assume" that these forces will be operated in a particular environment (desert, open plains, arctic conditions, etc.). Postulating other conditions or assumptions, however, could dramatically impact the assessment. Historically, US analysis of Soviet-Warsaw Pact operations against NATO had to "assume" a level of non-Soviet Warsaw Pact reliability (e.g., would these forces actually fight?). In this case, there was high uncertainty and depending on what level of reliability one assumed, the analyst could arrive at very different conclusions about a potential Soviet offensive operation. Or when economists assess the prospects for foreign economic reforms, they may consciously, or not, assume a degree of political stability in those countries or the region that may or may not exist in the future. Likewise, political analysts reviewing a developing country's domestic stability might unconsciously assume stable oil prices, when this key determinant of economic performance and underlying social peace might fluctuate. All of these examples highlight the fact that analysts often rely on stated and unstated assumptions to conduct their analysis. The goal is not to undermine or abandon key assumptions; rather, it is to make them explicit and identify what information or developments would demand rethinking them.

VALUE ADDED

Explicitly identifying working assumptions during an analytic project helps:

- Explain the logic of the analytic argument and expose faulty logic.

- Understand the key factors that shape an issue.

- Stimulate thinking about an issue.

- Uncover hidden relationships and links between key factors.

- Identify developments that would cause you to abandon an assumption.

- Prepare analysts for changed circumstances that could surprise them.

Key Assumptions Check: The 2002 DC Sniper Case

The outbreak of sniper shootings in the Washington, DC area in the fall of 2002 provides a good example of how this technique could have been applied. After the initial flurry of shootings, the operating assumption that quickly emerged was that the shootings were the work of a single, white male who had some military training and was driving a white van. If law enforcement officials had conducted a Key Assumptions Check, they could have broken this statement into its key components and assessed the validity of each statement as follows:

Key Assumption	Assessment
The sniper is a male.	Highly likely (but not certain) given past precedent with serial killers. We are taking little risk by not looking for a female.
The sniper is acting alone.	Highly likely (but not certain) given past precedents.
The sniper is white.	Likely, but not as certain, given past precedents. We would be taking some risk if we rule out nonwhites as suspects.
The sniper has military training/experience.	Possible, but not sufficient reason to exclude from consideration potential suspects who have not had any military training.
The sniper is driving a white van.	Possible because you have a credible eyewitness account but worthy of continuing scrutiny given the number of white vans in the area (more than 70,000 registered in the Maryland suburbs of Metropolitan Washington, DC) and that different kinds of vehicles are being described.

A Key Assumptions Check could have allowed law enforcement officials to:

- Avoid jumping to conclusions (the sniper is white, has military training, and is driving a white van) that did not hold up under closer scrutiny. By explicitly examining each assumption, officials could have avoided prematurely narrowing down the potential pool of suspects to a group that did not include the actual perpetrator. Similarly, they might have been more cautious about accepting that the sniper was driving a white van.

- Be receptive to new leads and citizen tips, such as eyewitness reports that the sniper fled the scene driving a specific model Chevrolet.

- More seriously consider evidence that subsequently became available, which contradicted a key assumption. If officials had stated explicitly that they were assuming the sniper was acting alone, they might have been sensitive to new information that contradicted that key assumption. Often this type of information gets "lost in the noise" if the analyst has not already thought about what key assumptions he or she is making.

THE METHOD

Checking for key assumptions requires analysts to consider how their analysis depends on the validity of certain premises, which they do not routinely question or believe to be in doubt. A four-step process will help analysts:

1. Review what the current analytic line on this issue appears to be; write it down for all to see.

2. Articulate all the premises, both stated and unstated in finished intelligence, which are accepted as true for this analytic line to be valid.

3. Challenge each assumption, asking why it "must" be true and whether it remains valid under all conditions.

4. Refine the list of key assumptions to contain only those that "must be true" to sustain your analytic line; consider under what conditions or in the face of what information these assumptions might not hold.

QUESTIONS TO ASK DURING THIS PROCESS INCLUDE:

- How much confidence exists that this assumption is correct?

- What explains the degree of confidence in the assumption?

- What circumstances or information might undermine this assumption?

- Is a key assumption more likely a key uncertainty or key factor?

- Could the assumption have been true in the past but less so now?

- If the assumption proves to be wrong, would it significantly alter the analytic line? How?

- Has this process identified new factors that need further analysis?

QUALITY OF INFORMATION CHECK

Evaluates completeness and soundness of available information sources.

WHEN TO USE

Weighing the validity of sources is a key feature of any critical thinking. Moreover, establishing how much confidence one puts in analytic judgments should ultimately rest on how accurate and reliable the information base is. Hence, checking the quality of information used in intelligence analysis is an ongoing, continuous process. Having multiple sources on an issue is not a substitute for having good information that has been thoroughly examined. Analysts should perform periodic checks of the information base for their analytic judgments. Otherwise, important analytic judgments can become anchored to weak information, and any "caveats" attached to those judgments in the past can be forgotten or ignored over time.

If a major analytic assessment is planned, analysts should individually or collectively review the quality of their information and refresh their understanding of the strengths and weaknesses of past reporting on which an analytic line rests. Without understanding the context and conditions under which critical information has been provided, it will be difficult for analysts to assess the information's validity and establish a confidence level in an intelligence assessment.

VALUE ADDED

A thorough review of information sources provides analysts—as well as policymakers—with an accurate assessment of "what we know" and "what we do not know." It is also an opportunity to confirm that sources have been cited accurately. In the case of HUMINT, this will require extensive review of the sources' background information and access as well as his or her motivation for providing the information. Similarly, reviewing technical sourcing can sometimes reveal inadvertent errors in processing, translation, or interpretation that otherwise might have gone unnoticed.

In addition, a quality of information check can be valuable to both collectors and policymakers:

- It can help to detect possible deception and denial strategies by an adversary.

- It can identify key intelligence gaps and new requirements for collectors.

- It can assist policymakers in understanding how much confidence analysts are placing on analytic judgments.

THE METHOD

An analyst or a team might begin a quality of information check by developing a database in which information is stored according to source type and date, with additional notations indicating strengths or weaknesses in those sources.[4] Ideally, analysts would have a retrieval and search capability on the database, so that periodic reviews are less labor intensive and result in a more complete review of all sources used in past analysis. For the information review to be fully effective, analysts will need as much background information on sources as is feasible. Knowing the circumstances in which reporting was obtained is often critical to understanding its validity. With the data in hand, analysts can then:

- Review systematically all sources for accuracy.

[4] Analysis of Competing Hypotheses (ACH), discussed later in the primer, is a useful technique for exploring the possibility that deception could explain the absence of evidence.

- Identify information sources that appear most critical or compelling.

- Check for sufficient and strong corroboration of critical reporting.

- Reexamine previously dismissed information in light of new facts or circumstances that cast it in a different light.

- Ensure that any recalled reporting is identified and properly flagged for other analysts; analysis based on recalled reporting should also be reviewed to determine if the reporting was essential to the judgments made.

- Consider whether ambiguous information has been interpreted and caveated properly.

- Indicate a level of confidence that analysts can place in sources, which are likely to figure in future analytic assessments.

Quality of Information Problem on Iraq

". . . Analysts community wide are unable to make fully informed judgments on the information they received, relying instead on nonspecific source lines to reach their assessments. Moreover, relevant operational data is nearly always withheld from analysts, putting them at a further analytical disadvantage . . ."

—Senate Select Committee on Intelligence, Report on the US Intelligence Community's Prewar Intelligence Assessments on Iraq

"Analytic errors included over-reliance on a single, ambiguous source, [and, in addition to collection shortfalls] failure of analysts to understand fully the limitations of technical collection . . ."

"The Intelligence Community relied too heavily on ambiguous imagery indicators . . ."

—Commission on the Intelligence Capabilities of the United States Regarding Weapons of Mass Destruction.

INDICATORS OR SIGNPOSTS OF CHANGE

Periodically review a list of observable events or trends to track events, monitor targets, spot emerging trends, and warn of unanticipated change.

WHEN TO USE

An analyst or team can create an indicators or signposts list of observable events that one would expect to see if a postulated situation is developing; e.g., economic reform, military modernization, political instability, or democratization. Constructing the list might require only a few hours or as much as several days to identify the critical variables associated with the targeted issue. The technique can be used whenever an analyst needs to track an event over time to monitor and evaluate changes. However, it can also be a very powerful aid in supporting other structured methods explained later in this primer. In those instances, analysts would be watching for mounting evidence to support a particular hypothesis, low-probability event, or scenario.

When there are sharply divided views on an issue, an indicators or signposts list can also "depersonalize" the argument by shifting analytic attention to a more objective set of criteria. Using an indicators list can clarify substantive disagreements, once all sides agree on the set of objective criteria used to measure the topic under study.

VALUE ADDED

By providing an objective baseline for tracking events or targets, indicators instill rigor into the analytic process and enhance the credibility of analytic judgments. An indicators list included in a finished product also allows the policymaker to track developments and builds a more concrete case for the analytic judgments. By laying out a list of critical variables, analysts also will be generating hypotheses regarding why they expect to see the presence of such factors. In so doing, analysts make the analytic line much more transparent and available for scrutiny by others.

THE METHOD

Whether used alone, or in combination with other structured analysis, the process is the same:

- Identify a set of competing hypotheses or scenarios.

- Create separate lists of potential activities, statements, or events expected for each hypothesis or scenario.

- Regularly review and update the indicators lists to see which are changing.

- Identify the most likely or most correct hypotheses or scenarios, based on the number of changed indicators that are observed.

Developing two lists of indicators for each hypothesis or scenario may prove useful to distinguish between indicators that a development is or is not emerging. This is particularly useful in a "What If?" Analysis, when it is important to make a case that a certain event is unlikely to happen.

Tracking the Potential for Political Instability in a Foreign Country

Topics	Indicators	1999				2000		
		I	*II*	*III*	*IV*	*I*	*II*	*III*
Government Capacity	Quality of leadership/organizational capabilities	●	●	●	■	●	●	●
	Responsiveness to popular demands	●	●	●	●	●	●	●
	Ability to deliver basic goods and services							
	Internal Security Capabilities							
	Effectiveness of civil/criminal justice systems							
Legitimacy of Regime	Breadth and depth of political participation	●	●	●	●	●	●	●
	Perceived level of corruption	●	●	●	●	●	●	●
	Human rights violations	●	●	●	●	●	●	●
	Weakness of civil society							
	Pervasiveness of transnational criminal organizations							
	External support for government							
Opposition Activity	Ethnic/religious discontent	●	●	●	●	●	●	●
	Military discontent with civilian government	●	●	●	●	●	●	●
	Popular demonstrations/strikes/riots							
	Insurgent/separatist/terrorist group activity							
	External support for opposition							
	Threat of conflict with or in neighboring state							
Economic Factors	Weakness of domestic economy/unemployment/inflation							
	Degree of income disparity							
	Capital flight							
	Decreased access to foreign funds							
	Reduced trade openness							
Environmental Issues	Extent of environmental degradation							
	Food/energy shortages							
	Ability to respond to natural disasters							

Presence of Trigger Mechanisms (▶ if present)

Contested elections	▶
Unpopular changes in food/energy prices	▶
Sudden imposition of unpopular policies	
Coup plotting	▶
Government mismanagement of natural disaster or national emergency	
Death of key figure	

■ Serious concern
● Substantial concern
● Moderate concern
● Low concern
● Negligible concern

Tracking the Potential for Political Instability in an Indicators Matrix. Analysts tracked the potential for regime change in 2000 and identified a list of indicators, to which they posed the question, "is this occurring or not? Analysts also went further and developed a list of "trigger mechanisms" that might bring about a political shift.

ANALYSIS OF COMPETING HYPOTHESES (ACH)

Identification of alternative explanations (hypotheses) and evaluation of all evidence that will disconfirm rather than confirm hypotheses.

WHEN TO USE

Analysis of Competing Hypotheses (ACH) has proved to be a highly effective technique when there is a large amount of data to absorb and evaluate. While a single analyst can use ACH, it is most effective with a small team that can challenge each other's evaluation of the evidence. Developing a matrix of hypotheses and loading already collected information into the matrix can be accomplished in a day or less. If the data must be reassembled, the initial phases of the ACH process may require additional time. Sometimes a facilitator or someone familiar with the technique can lead new analysts through this process for the first time.

ACH is particularly appropriate for controversial issues when analysts want to develop a clear record that shows what theories they have considered and how they arrived at their judgments. Developing the ACH matrix allows other analysts (or even policymakers) to review their analysis and identify areas of agreement and disagreement. Evidence can also be examined more systematically, and analysts have found that this makes the technique ideal for considering the possibility of deception and denial.

VALUE ADDED

ACH helps analysts overcome three common mistakes that can lead to inaccurate forecasts:

- Analysts often are susceptible to being unduly influenced by a first impression, based on incomplete data, an existing analytic line, or a single explanation that seems to fit well enough.

- Analysts seldom generate a full set of explanations or hypotheses at the outset of a project.

- Analysts often rely on evidence to support their preferred hypothesis, but which also is consistent with other explanations.

In essence, ACH helps analysts to avoid picking the first solution that seems satisfactory instead of going through all the possibilities to arrive at the very best solution.

THE METHOD

ACH demands that analysts explicitly identify all the reasonable alternative hypotheses, then array the evidence against each hypothesis—rather than evaluating the plausibility of each hypothesis one at a time. To create a level playing field, the process must:

- Ensure that all the information and argumentation is evaluated and given equal treatment or weight when considering each hypothesis.

- Prevent the analyst from premature closure on a particular explanation or hypothesis.

- Protect the analyst against innate tendencies to ignore or discount information that does not fit comfortably with the preferred explanation at the time.

To accomplish this, the process should follow these steps:

- Brainstorm among analysts with different perspectives to identify all possible hypotheses.

- List all significant evidence and arguments relevant to all the hypotheses.

- Prepare a matrix with hypotheses across the top and each piece of evidence on the side. Determine whether each piece of evidence is consistent, inconsistent, or not applicable to each hypothesis.[5]

- Refine the matrix and reconsider the hypotheses—in some cases, analysts will need to add new hypotheses and re-examine the information available.

- Focus on disproving hypotheses rather than proving one. Talley the pieces of evidence that are inconsistent and consistent with each hypothesis to see which explanations are the weakest and strongest.

- Analyze how sensitive the ACH results are to a few critical items of evidence; should those pieces prove to be wrong, misleading, or subject to deception, how would it impact an explanation's validity?

- Ask what evidence is not being seen but would be expected for a given hypothesis to be true. Is denial and deception a possibility?

- Report all the conclusions, including the weaker hypotheses that should still be monitored as new information becomes available.

- Establish the relative likelihood for the hypotheses and report all the conclusions, including the weaker hypotheses that should still be monitored as new information becomes available.

- Identify and monitor indicators that would be both consistent and inconsistent with the full set of hypotheses. In the latter case, explore what could account for inconsistent data.

[5] The "diagnostic value" of the evidence will emerge as analysts determine whether a piece of evidence is found to be consistent with only one hypothesis, or could support more than one or indeed all hypotheses. In the latter case, the evidence can be judged as unimportant to determining which hypothesis is more likely correct.

Terrorism in Tokyo From Aum Shinrikyo

		Weight	H: 1 Kooky Cult	H: 4 Terrorist Group	H: 2 Political Movement	H: 3 Criminal Group
	Inconsistency Score		-1.0	-1.0	-2.0	-3.0
E3	Attacks on Journalists	MEDIUM	I	N	I	I
E2	Religious Affiliation	MEDIUM	C	I	I	I
E4	Established Party	MEDIUM	N	N	C	I
E1	Blind Leader Mastsumoto	MEDIUM	C	C	C	C

ACH Matrix of Terrorism in Tokyo. In March 1995, a largely unknown group attacked the Tokyo subways by using a highly lethal nerve agent known as sarin. ACH provides a mechanism to carefully examine all the evidence and possible explanations for understanding what type of group could have been responsible. In simplified form, the above matrix arrays each piece of evidence on the vertical axis and then evaluates each in terms of the item's consistency with four possible explanations for the terrorist attack in Tokyo (horizontal axis). Analysts rate a piece of evidence as consistent (C); inconsistent (I); or neutral (N). This process allows analysts to see that some evidence will be consistent with more than one hypothesis and be less valuable in disproving hypotheses.

DEVIL'S ADVOCACY

Challenging a single, strongly held view or consensus by building the best possible case for an alternative explanation.

WHEN TO USE

Devil's Advocacy is most effective when used to challenge an analytic consensus or a key assumption regarding a critically important intelligence question. On those issues that one cannot afford to get wrong, Devil's Advocacy can provide further confidence that the current analytic line will hold up to close scrutiny. An individual analyst can often assume the role of the Devil's Advocate if he or she has some doubts about a widely held view, or a manager might designate a courageous analyst to challenge the prevailing wisdom in order to reaffirm the group's confidence in those judgments. In some cases, the analyst or a team can review a key assumption of a critical judgment in the course of their work, or more likely, a separate analytic product can be generated that arrays all the arguments and data that support a contrary hypothesis. While this can involve some analytic time and effort, when a group of analysts have worked on an issue for a long period of time, it is probably wise to assume that a strong mind-set exists that deserves the closer scrutiny provided by Devil's Advocacy.

VALUE ADDED

Analysts have an obligation to policymakers to understand where their own analytic judgments might be weak and open to future challenge. Hence, the Devil's Advocacy process can highlight weaknesses in a current analytic judgment or alternatively help to reaffirm one's confidence in the prevailing judgments by:

- Explicitly challenging key assumptions to see if they will not hold up under some circumstances.

- Identifying any faulty logic or information that would undermine the key analytic judgments.

- Presenting alternative hypotheses that would explain the current body of information available to analysts.

Its primary value is to serve as a check on a dominant mind-set that can develop over time among even the best analysts who have followed an issue and formed strong consensus that there is only one way of looking at their issue. This mind-set phenomenon makes it more likely that contradictory evidence is dismissed or not given proper weight or consideration. An exercise aimed at highlighting such evidence and proposing another way of thinking about an issue can expose hidden assumptions and compel analysts to review their information with greater skepticism about their findings. The analyst could come away from the exercise more certain that: 1) the current analytic line was sound; 2) the argument is still the strongest, but that there are areas where further analysis is needed; or 3) some serious flaws in logic or supporting evidence suggest that the analytic line needs to be changed or at least caveated more heavily.

THE METHOD

To challenge the prevailing analytic line, the Devil's Advocate must:

- Outline the mainline judgment and key assumptions and characterize the evidence supporting that current analytic view.

- Select one or more assumptions—stated or not—that appear the most susceptible to challenge.

- Review the information used to determine whether any is of questionable validity, whether deception is possibly indicated, or whether major gaps exist.

- Highlight the evidence that could support an alternative hypothesis or contradicts the current thinking.

- Present to the group the findings that demonstrate there are flawed assumptions, poor quality evidence, or possible deception at work.

- Consider drafting a separate contrarian paper that lays out the arguments for a different analytic conclusion if the review uncovers major analytic flaws.

- Be sure that any products generated clearly lay out the conventional wisdom and are identified as an explicitly "Devil's Advocate" project; otherwise, the reader can become confused as to the current official view on the issue.

TEAM A/TEAM B

Use of separate analytic teams that contrast two (or more) strongly held views or competing hypotheses.

WHEN TO USE

A Team A/Team B approach is different from Devil's Advocacy, where the purpose is to challenge a single dominant mind-set. Instead, Team A/Team B recognizes that there may be competing and possibly equally strong mind-sets held on an issue that need to be clarified. Sometimes analysts confuse the two techniques by drafting a Team B exercise that is really a Devil's Advocacy exercise.

If there are at least two competing views within an analytic office or perhaps competing opinions within the policymaking community on a key issue, then Team A/Team B analysis can be the appropriate technique to use. Developing a full-blown Team A/Team B exercise requires a significant commitment of analytic time and resources, so it is worthwhile considering if the analytic issue merits this kind of attention.

A longstanding policy issue, a critical decision that has far-reaching implications, or a dispute within the analytic community that has obstructed effective cross-agency cooperation would be grounds for using Team A/Team B. If those circumstances exist, then analysts will need to review all of the data to develop alternative papers that can capture the essential differences between the two viewpoints.

VALUE ADDED

Managers have found that when there are office tensions among competing factions of analysts, a Team A/Team B approach can help opposing experts see the merit in the other group's perspective. The process of conducting such an exercise can reduce the friction and even narrow the differences. At a minimum, it allows those holding opposing views to feel that their views have been given equal attention.

For the policymaker, this technique helps to surface and explain important analytic differences within the expert community. Often senior officials can learn more by weighing well-argued conflicting views than from reading an assessment that masks substantive differences or drives analysis to the lowest common denominator. By making the key assumptions and information used for each argument more transparent, a policymaker can judge the merits of each case, pose questions back to the analysts, and reach an independent judgment on which argument is the strongest. Moreover, highlighting alternative views puts collectors on notice that they need to be searching for new information that can confirm or disconfirm a range of hypotheses.

If opposing positions are well established, it can be useful to place analysts on teams that will advocate positions they normally do not support; forcing analysts to argue "the other side" can often make them more aware of their own mind-set.

A Team A/Team B View: China's Military

A: *China's Hollow Military* by Bates Gill and Michael O'Hanlon	B: *China's Military: A Second Opinion* by James Lilley and Carl Ford
". . . We believe that the recent clamor over China's strategic ambitions is greatly overblown. Most of the Chinese aims that run counter to US interests are in fact not global or ideological but territorial in nature and confined primarily to the islands and waterways to China's south and southeast . . . An enormous gap separates China's military capabilities from its aspirations. The PRC's armed forces are not very good and not getting better very fast. Whatever China's concerns and intentions, its capacity to act upon them in ways inimical to US interests is severely limited, and will remain so for many years . . . The PRC's power projection capabilities, too, are constrained by huge weaknesses—especially in areas such as aerial refueling, electronic warfare, command and control and amphibious and air assault assets. China owns considerably less top-level equipment than medium powers like Japan and Britain; it owns even less than smaller powers such as Italy, South Korea or The Netherlands . . . The resources it devotes to acquiring modern weaponry are akin to those of countries spending $10-20 billion a year on defense . . ."	". . . We think they got it half right. China is no military superpower and will not acquire that status for some years to come. But measured in terms of its capacity to challenge key US allies in East Asia, China's capabilities have grown exponentially . . . By emphasizing direct comparisons between the defense capabilities of the United States and the PRC, the authors create an artificial and misleading construct . . . What the regime gives every indication of striving for is sufficient military clout to achieve its aims in Asia. In the short term, it wishes to intimidate Taiwan sufficiently to bring about unification on Beijing's terms . . . . . . Investments of the sort Beijing is making can mean only one thing: China is determined to improve the PLA's fighting capability. While most nations are reducing defense expenditures in the post–Cold War era, China is one of the few doing the opposite . . . Across the board, the PLA is engaged in a major spending effort to upgrade weapons and equipment and improve its operational capability. According to the Pentagon, these efforts have already enhanced China's ability to project military power . . ."

—*Excerpted from journal articles found in The National Interest, Fall and Winter 2000/2001.*

THE METHOD

Analysis Phase. A Team A/Team B exercise can be conducted on an important issue to:

- Identify the two (or more) competing hypotheses or points of view.

- Form teams or designate individuals to develop the best case that can be made for each hypothesis.

- Review all pertinent information that supports their respective positions.

- Identify missing information that would buttress their hypotheses.

- Structure each argument with an explicit presentation of key assumptions, key pieces of evidence, and careful articulation of the logic behind the argument.

Debate Phase. An oral presentation of the alternative arguments and rebuttals in parallel fashion can then be organized for the benefit of other analysts:

- Set aside time for an oral presentation of the alternative team findings; this can an informal brainstorming session or a more formal "debate."

- Have an independent "jury of peers" listen to the oral presentation and be prepared to question the teams regarding their assumptions, evidence, or logic.

- Allow each team to present their case, challenge the other team's arguments, and rebut the opponent's critique of its case.

- Let the jury consider the strength of each presentation and recommend possible next steps for further research and collection efforts.

HIGH-IMPACT/LOW-PROBABILITY ANALYSIS

Highlights a seemingly unlikely event that would have major policy consequences if it happened.

WHEN TO USE

High-Impact/Low-Probability Analysis is a contrarian technique that sensitizes analysts to the potential impact of seemingly low probability events that would have major repercussions on US interests. Using this technique is advisable when analysts and policymakers are convinced that an event is unlikely but have not given much thought to the consequences of its occurrence. In essence, this can be a warning that the intelligence and policy communities must be alert to an unexpected but not impossible event. For example, the fall of the Shah, the collapse of the Soviet Union, and the reunification of Germany were all considered low probability events at one time; however, analysts might have benefited from considering the consequences of such events and how they might plausibly have come about.

VALUE ADDED

Mapping out the course of an unlikely, yet plausible, event can uncover hidden relationships between key factors and assumptions; it also can alert analysts to oversights in the mainstream analytic line. In addition, an examination of the "unthinkable" allows analysts to develop signposts that may provide early warning of a shift in the situation. By periodically reviewing these indicators an analyst is more likely to counter any prevailing mind-set that such a development is highly unlikely.

THE METHOD

If there is a strongly held view that an event is unlikely, then postulating precisely the opposite should not be difficult.

- Define the high-impact outcome clearly. This process is what will justify examining what most analysts believe to be a very unlikely development.

- Devise one or more plausible explanations for or "pathways" to the low probability outcome. This should be as precise as possible, as it can help identify possible indicators for later monitoring.

- Insert possible triggers or changes in momentum if appropriate. These can be natural disasters, sudden health problems of key leaders, or new economic or political shocks that might have occurred historically or in other parts of the world.

- Brainstorm with analysts having a broad set of experiences to aid the development of plausible but unpredictable triggers of sudden change.

- Identify for each pathway a set of indicators or "observables" that would help you anticipate that events were beginning to play out this way.

- Identify factors that would deflect a bad outcome or encourage a positive outcome.

High Impact of a Low-Probability Event: Pearl Harbor

". . . So far as relations directly between the United States and Japan are concerned, there is less reason today than there was a week ago for the United States to be apprehensive lest Japan make "war" on this country.

Were it a matter of placing bets, the undersigned would give odds of five to one that the United States and Japan will not be at "war" on or before December 15; would wager three to one that the United States and Japan will not be at 'war' on or before the 15th of January (i.e, seven weeks from now); would wager even money that the United States and Japan will not be at "war" on or before March 1 (a date more than 90 days from now) . . ."

—*State Department Special Assessment, 27 November 1941*

High-Impact/Low-Probability Analysis on 9/11

The 9/11 Commission report includes examination of speculative analysis that was provided to senior policymakers highlighting what were thought to be highly unlikely scenarios that would have a very high impact. One of those items was the 6 August 2001 President's Daily Brief, which stated:

Al-Qai'da members—including some who are US citizens—have resided in or traveled to the US for years, and the group apparently maintains a support structure that could aid attacks. Two al-Qai'da members found guilty in the conspiracy to bomb our embassies in East Africa were US citizens, and a senior EIJ [Egyptian Islamic Jihad] member lived in California in the mid-1990s.

- A clandestine source said in 1998 that a Bin Ladin cell in New York was recruiting Muslim-American youth for attacks.

We have not been able to corroborate some of the more sensational threat reporting, such as that from a service in 1998 saying that Bin Ladin wanted to hijack a US aircraft to gain the release of "Blind Shaykh" 'Umar Abd al-Rahman and other US-held extremists.

—*9/11 Commission Report, declassified and approved for release 10 April 2004.*

"WHAT IF?" ANALYSIS

Assumes that an event has occurred with potential (negative or positive) impact and explains how it might come about.

WHEN TO USE

"What If?" analysis is another contrarian technique for challenging a strong mind-set that an event will not happen or that a confidently made forecast may not be entirely justified. It is similar to a High-Impact/Low-Probability analysis, but it does not dwell on the consequences of the event as much as it accepts the significance and moves directly to explaining how it might come about.

VALUE ADDED

By shifting the focus from whether an event could occur to how it may happen, analysts allow themselves to suspend judgment about the likelihood of the event and focus more on what developments—even unlikely ones—might enable such an outcome. An individual analyst or a team might employ this technique and repeat the exercise whenever a critical analytic judgment is made.

Using this technique is particularly important when a judgment rests on limited information or unproven assumptions. Moreover, it can free analysts from arguing about the probability of an event to considering its consequences and developing some indicators or signposts for its possible emergence. It will help analysts address the impact of an event, the factors that could cause—or alter—it, and likely signposts that an event is imminent.

A "What If?" analysis can complement a difficult judgment reached and provide the policymaker a thoughtful caution to accepting the conventional wisdom without considering the costs and risks of being wrong. This can help decision-makers consider ways to hedge their bets, even if they accept the analytic judgment that an event remains unlikely.

THE METHOD

Like other contrarian methods, "What If?" analysis must begin by stating clearly the conventional analytic line and then stepping back to consider what alternative outcomes are too important to dismiss, even if unlikely. Brainstorming over a few days or weeks can develop one or more plausible scenarios by which the unlikely event occurs:

- Assume the event has happened.

- Select some triggering events that permitted the scenario to unfold to help make the "what if" more plausible; for example, analysts might postulate the death of a leader, a natural disaster, or some economic event that would start a chain of other events.

- Develop a chain of argumentation based as much on logic as evidence to explain how this outcome could have come about.

- "Think backwards" from the event in concrete ways–that is, specifying what must actually occur at each stage of the scenario is often very useful.

- Identify one or more plausible pathways or scenarios to the unlikely event; very often more than one will appear possible.

- Generate a list of indicators or "observables" for each scenario that would help to detect the beginnings of the event.

- Consider the scope of the positive and negative consequences of each scenario and their relative impacts.

- Monitor the indicators developed on a periodic basis.

"What If?" Analysis: An Unlikely Outcome in Yugoslavia, 1990.

The possibility of muddling through is very low. In the unlikely event that it happens, this is what it would look like.

Memories of the internecine civil war during World War II and fear of another destructive conflict would lead the two most numerous South Slav people—Serbs and Croats—to reach some political accommodation. A compromise that preserves Yugoslavia would include:

• Basic principles:
  -No change in existing Republic borders.
  -No change in Yugoslavia's existing international status.
  -Mutually recognized sovereignty of each republic

• Confederal institutions:
  -A single foreign ministry, to which diplomatic representatives would be accredited.
  -A central military organization with a joint General Staff responsible for planning.
  -A central bank, determining macroeconomic policy, a common currency,

• Powers reserved to republics.
  -Veto over actions of the Confederal Authority.
  -Control of internal security, including guarantee of minority rights.
  -Operational control over some or all military units stationed on the republic's territory.
  -Raising taxes and allocating funds to discharge mutually agreed confederal responsibilities.

Only the Serbs can open the door to a confederal Yugoslavia, and Serbia's leader, Slobodan Milosevic, holds the key. Some observers felt there are pressures on him to try. If he does not, he would give his opponents the leverage to remove him. The potential penalties of failure to compromise would be too great, in this view, for the peoples and leaders of Yugoslavia to forgo every effort to find a compromise.

—*Excerpts from the declassified* NIE: Prospects for Yugoslavia, *October 1990.*

BRAINSTORMING

An unconstrained group process designed to generate new ideas and concepts.

WHEN TO USE

Brainstorming is a widely used technique for stimulating new thinking and it can be applied to virtually all of the other structured analysis techniques as an aid to thinking. Typically, analytic will brainstorm when they begin a project to help generate a range of hypotheses about their issue.

Brainstorming, almost by definition, involves a group of analysts meeting to discuss a common challenge; a modest investment of time at the beginning or critical points of a project can take advantage of their different perspectives to help structure a problem. This group process allows others to build on an initial idea suggested by a member of the brainstorming session.

An individual analyst also can brainstorm to produce a wider range of ideas than a group might generate, without regard for other analysts' egos, opinions, or objections. However, an individual will not have the benefit of others' perspectives to help develop the ideas as fully. Moreover, an individual may have difficulty breaking free of his or her cognitive biases without the benefit of a diverse group.

VALUE ADDED

This technique can maximize creativity in the thinking process, force analysts to step outside their normal analytic mind-sets, and suspend their typical "good judgment" about the practicality of ideas or approaches. More generally, brainstorming allows analysts to see a wider range of factors that might bear on the topic than they would otherwise consider. Analysts typically censor out ideas that seem farfetched, poorly sourced, or seemingly irrelevant to the question at hand. Brainstorming gives permission to think more radically or "outside the box." In particular, it can spark new ideas, ensure a comprehensive look at a problem or issues, raise unknowns, and prevent premature consensus around a single hypothesis.

THE METHOD

Paradoxically, brainstorming should be a very structured process to be most productive. An unconstrained, informal discussion might produce some interesting ideas, but usually a more systematic process is the most effective way to break down mind-sets and produce new insights. In particular, the process involves a divergent thinking phase to generate and collect new ideas and insights, followed by a convergent phase in which ideas are grouped and organized around key concepts. Some of the simple rules to be followed include:

- Never censor an analyst's ideas no matter how unconventional they might sound.

- Rather find out what prompted the thought, as it might contain the seeds of an important connection between the topic and an unstated assumption.

- Give yourself enough time to do brainstorming correctly. It usually takes one hour to set the "rules" of the game, get the group comfortable, and exhaust the conventional wisdom on the topic. Only then will the truly creative ideas begin to emerge.

- Involve at least one "outsider" in the process—that is, someone who does not share the same educational background, culture, technical knowledge or mind-set as the core group but has some familiarity with the topic.

A two-phase, twelve-step, structured process is often used to get the most out of the brainstorming sessions:

Brainstorming and Divergent Thinking:
Perspectives of an Experienced Practitioner

". . . First, leave rank at the door and focus on "a democracy of ideas." Thoughts from experts, senior officers, and supervisors are of course, valuable and welcome, but such experts are not permitted to cut off debate by citing their seniority. In fact, it pays to invite junior officers as well as senior ones who are not involved directly in working the issue under discussion. Some of the most creative ideas at brainstorming sessions frequently come from relatively junior people who can look at a problem with fresh perspective, or from senior ones who are not experts on the issue.

Second, make sure there is no official analytic line. One of the most significant blocks to new thinking is the presence of a long held analytic line that analysts—and even more so managers—are reluctant to change. Rather than trying to fit ideas into the framework of "what we've said before," analysts need to feel free to go wherever bits of the evidence and informed supposition take them. They must feel free to throw out seemingly strange but plausible ideas that might be based on historical precedent and instinct rather than on concrete information. Facilitators can stimulate this process by deliberately posing an alternative outcome to a problem that differs starkly from the accepted analysis or by proposing a contrary way to think about an issue.

Third, don't permit killer phrases like "that would not work" or "that could not happen" to be voiced out loud. Effective brainstorming starts with ideas and possibilities, not with practicalities and self-imposed obstacles to fresh perspectives. Force the group to get as wide a range of ideas out for discussion as possible. At some point, a set of ideas might be winnowed down and subject to tests of workability, but that comes later—not during brainstorming.

Fourth, keep the brainstorming session to no more than 90 minutes. There is no hard and fast rule, but somewhere between 60 and 90 minutes, the idea stream starts to dry up, people repeat themselves, and jokes replace creative ideas.

Fifth, record ideas in a visible way. Lots of people take notes at brainstorming sessions for their own use, and that is good. We have found it valuable to have someone jot down the ideas presented on large paste-a-note sheets that we put on the walls. This allows participants in brainstorming sessions to react to ideas generated earlier. Moreover, analysts are encouraged to participate in such exercises if they see their own ideas put down in writing. Having a notional record of brainstorming also helps the analyst who ends up writing a report based on the discussion. Ideas that may not be used in one report are invariably put to use later, so it is good to have a record of them . . ."

Divergent Thinking Phase:

- Distribute "Post-It" notes and pens or markers to all participants. Typically, 10-12 people works best.

- Pose the problem in terms of a "focal question." Display it in one sentence on a large easel or whiteboard.

- Ask the group to write down responses to the question, using key words that will fit on the small "Post-It" note.

- Stick all the notes on a wall for all to see—treat all ideas the same.

- When a pause follows the initial flow of ideas, the group is reaching the end of their conventional thinking and the new divergent ideas are then likely to emerge.

- End the "collection stage" of the brainstorming after two or three pauses.

Convergent Thinking Phase:

- Ask the participants as a group to rearrange the notes on the wall according to their commonalities or similar concepts. No talking is permitted. Some notes may be moved several times as notes begin to cluster. Copying some notes is permitted to allow ideas to be included in more than one group.

- Select a word or phrase that characterizes each grouping or cluster once all the notes have been arranged.

- Identify any notes that do not easily fit with others and consider them either useless noise or the beginning of an idea that deserves further attention.

- Assess what the group has accomplished in terms of new ideas or concepts identified or new areas that need more work or further brainstorming.

- Instruct each participant to select one or two areas that deserve the most attention. Tabulate the votes.

- Set the brainstorming group's priorities based on the voting and decide on the next steps for analysis.

OUTSIDE-IN THINKING

Used to identify the full range of basic forces, factors, and trends that would indirectly shape an issue.

WHEN TO USE

Analysts find this technique most useful at the conceptualization of an analytic project, when the goal is to identify all the critical, external factors that could influence how a particular situation will develop. It would work well for a group of analysts responsible for a range of functional and/or regional issues. When assembling a large database that must identify a number of information categories or database fields, this technique can aid in visualizing the entire set of categories that might be needed in a research effort. Often analysts realize only too late that some additional information categories will be needed and then must go back and review all previous files and recode the data. With a modest amount of effort, "Outside-in Thinking" can reduce the risk of missing important variables early in the analytic process.

VALUE ADDED

Most analysts spend their time concentrating on familiar factors within their field or analytic issue. That is, they think from the "inside"—namely, what they control—out to the broader world. Conversely, "thinking from the outside-in" begins by considering the external changes that might, over time, profoundly affect the analysts' own field or issue. This technique encourages analysts to get away from their immediate analytic tasks (the so-called "inbox") and think about their issues in a wider conceptual

and contextual framework. By recasting the problem in much broader and fundamental terms, analysts are more likely to uncover additional factors, an important dynamic, or a relevant alternative hypothesis.

THE METHOD

The process begins by developing a generic description of the problem or the phenomenon under study. Then, analysts should:

- List all the key forces (social, technological, economic, environmental, and political) that could have an impact on the topic, but over which one can exert little influence (e.g., globalization, social stress, the Internet, or the global economy).

- Focus next on key factors over which an actor or policymaker can exert some influence. In the business world this might be the market size, customers, the competition, suppliers or partners; in the government domain it might include the policy actions or the behavior of allies or adversaries.

- Assess how each of these forces could affect the analytic problem.

- Determine whether these forces actually do have an impact on the particular issue based on the available evidence.

RED TEAM ANALYSIS

Models the behavior of an individual or group by trying to replicate how an adversary would think about an issue.

WHEN TO USE

Frequently, analysts face the challenge of forecasting how a foreign leader or decisionmaking group may behave when it is clear that there is a risk of falling into a "mirror-image" problem. That is, analysts can sometimes impute to a foreign actor the same motives, values, or understanding of an issue that they hold. Traditional analysis sometimes assumes that foreign leaders or groups will behave "rationally" and act as the analysts would if faced with the same threats or opportunities. History has shown that foreign leaders often respond differently to events because of different cultural, organizational, or personal experiences.

Red Team analysis tries to consciously place analysts in the same cultural, organizational, and personal setting ("putting them in their shoes") in which the target individual or group operates. Whereas analysts normally work from the position of the "blue" (friendly forces), a "red" team of analysts attempts to work in the environment of the hostile forces.

VALUE ADDED

Like Devil's Advocacy and Team A/Team B techniques, Red Team analysis is aimed at freeing the analyst from the prison of a well-developed mind-set; in this case, the analyst's own sense of rationality, cultural norms, and personal values. Whereas analysts usually operate as "observers" of a foreign adversary, the Red Team technique transforms the analyst into an "actor" operating within the adversary's culture and political milieu. This form of "role playing" is useful when trying to replicate the mind-set of authoritarian leaders, terrorist cells, or other non-Western groups that operate under very different codes of behavior or motivations.

Often this technique can introduce new or different stimuli that might not have been factored into traditional analysis—such as the target's familial ties or the international political, economic, and military pressures felt by the individual. For example, Red Team participants might ask themselves: "What would my peers, family, or tribe expect me to do? Alternatively, a Red Team analyst might pose the question to his colleagues: "How do we perceive the external threats and opportunities?" Finally, the Red Team technique can factor into its analysis the way in which personal power and status might influence a target's behavior.

THE METHOD

On issues that lend themselves to Red Team analysis, a manager needs to build a team of experts with in-depth knowledge of the operating environment, the target's personality, and the style of thinking used. The team should be populated not just with those who understand the language, but also with people who might have experienced the culture, share the ethnic background, or have worked in a similar operational environment. Once established and separated from traditional analysis, the team members should:

• Put themselves in the adversary's circumstances and react to foreign stimuli as the target would.

• Develop a set of "first-person" questions that the adversary would ask, such as: "How would I perceive incoming information; what would be my personal concerns; or to whom would I look for an opinion?"

• Draft a set of policy papers in which the leader or group makes specific decisions, proposes recommendations, or lays out courses of actions. The more these papers reflect the cultural and personal norms of the target, the more they can offer a different perspective on the analytic problem.

A Red Team Perspective
Iran's Military Strategy Vis-a-vis the United States

". . . The United States and Israel may be contemplating military operations against Iran, as per recent media reports . . . A week-long combined air and ground maneuver has just concluded in five of the southern and western provinces of Iran, mesmerizing foreign observers, who have described as 'spectacular' the massive display of high-tech, mobile operations, including rapid-deployment forces relying on squadrons of helicopters, air lifts, missiles, as well as hundreds of tanks and tens of thousands of well-coordinated personnel using live munitions.

Learning from both the 2003 Iraq war and Iran's own previous experiences of the 1980-88 war with Iraq and the 1987-88 confrontation with US forces in the Persian Gulf, Iranians have focused on the merits of a fluid and complex defensive strategy that seeks to take advantage of certain weaknesses in the US military superpower while maximizing the precious few areas where they may have the upper hand, e.g.; numerical superiority in ground forces, guerrilla tactics, terrain, etc.

Any US attack on Iran will likely be met first and foremost by missile counter-attacks engulfing the southern Persian Gulf states playing host to US forces, as well as any other country—e.g., Azerbaijan, Iraq, or Turkey allowing their territory or airspace to be used against Iran. The rationale for this strategy is precisely to pre-warn Iran's neighbors of the dire consequences, with potential debilitating impacts on their economies for a long time, should they become accomplices of foreign invaders of Iran.

Another key element of Iran's strategy is to "increase the arch of crisis" in places such as Afghanistan and Iraq, where it has considerable influence, to undermine the United States' foothold in the region, hoping to create a counter-domino effect wherein instead of gaining inside Iran, the US would actually lose territory partly as a result of thinning its forces and military 'overreach.'

Iran's counter-psychological warfare, on the other hand, seeks to take advantage of the 'death-fearing' American soldiers who typically lack a strong motivation to fight wars not necessarily in defense of the homeland. A war with Iran would definitely require establishing the draft in the US, without which it could not possibly protect its flanks in Afghanistan and Iraq.

There is a sense of national-security siege in Iran these days, in light of a tightening "security belt" by the US benefiting from military bases in Iraq, Turkey, Azerbaijan, Uzbekistan, Tajikistan, Kyrgyzstan, as well as Kuwait, Saudi Arabia, Qatar, Bahrain, Oman, and the island-turned garrison of Diego Garcia. From Iran's vantage point, the US, having won the Cold War, has turned into a 'leviathan unhinged' capable of manipulating and subverting the rule of international law and the United Nations with impunity, thus requiring a sophisticated Iranian strategy of deterrence, that, in the words of certain Iranian media pundits, would even include the use of nuclear weapons . . ."

—*Excerpts from Kaveh L. Afrasiabi (Tehran University), "How Iran Will Fight Back," cited in Asia Times Online Ltd., 2004.*

Red Team analysis is not easy to conduct. It requires significant time to develop a team of qualified experts who can think like the adversary. The team has to distance itself from the normal analysis and work as though living in the target's world. Without a sophisticated understanding of the culture, operational environment, and personal histories of the foreign group, analysts will not be able to behave or think like the enemy. Analysts can never truly escape their own experiences and mind-sets, but this technique can at least prevent them from falling into "mirror-imaging" unconsciously.

The most novel feature of Red Team analysis is its presentation.

- The analysis is often in a "first person" format—that is, drafted as memos to or from a leader or group.

- Red Team analysis avoids the use of caveats or qualifications and assumes that the recipient understands that the paper is aimed more at provoking thought or challenging the conventional understanding of how an adversary thinks.

- Such papers are rarely coordinated among other experts and do not purport to represent the consensus view on an issue.

Red Team papers do not plot out all possible courses of action but seek to give a prediction based on the target's special personal, organizational, or cultural experiences.

ALTERNATIVE FUTURES ANALYSIS

Systematically explores multiple ways a situation can develop when there is high complexity and uncertainty.

WHEN TO USE
Alternative futures analysis (often referred to as "scenarios") is most useful when a situation is viewed as too complex or the outcomes as too uncertain to trust a single outcome assessment. First, analysts must recognize that there is high uncertainty surrounding the topic in question. Second, they, and often their customers, recognize that they need to consider a wide range of factors that might bear on the question. And third, they are prepared to explore a range of outcomes and are not wedded to any preconceived result. Depending on how elaborate the futures project, the effort can amount to considerable investment in time, analytic resources, and money. A team of analysts can spend several hours or days organizing, brainstorming, and developing multiple futures; alternatively, a larger-scale effort can require preparing a multi-day workshop that brings together participants (including outside experts). Such an undertaking often demands the special skills of trained scenario-development facilitators and conferencing facilities.

This technique is a sharp contrast to contrarian techniques, which try to challenge the analysts' high confidence and relative certitude about an event or trend. Instead, multiple futures development is a divergent thinking technique that tries to use the complexity and uncertainty of a situation to describe multiple outcomes or futures that the analyst and policymaker should consider, rather than to predict one outcome.

VALUE ADDED
Alternative futures analysis is extremely useful in highly ambiguous situations, when analysts confront not only a lot of "known unknowns" but also "unknown unknowns." What this means is that analysts recognize that there are factors, forces, and dynamics among key actors that are difficult to identify without the use of some structured technique that can model how they would interact or behave. As the outcomes are not known prior to the futures exercise, analysts must be prepared for the unexpected and willing to engage in a more free-wheeling exchange of views than typically occurs in order to "imagine the future." Given the time and resources involved, scenario analysis is best reserved for situations that could potentially pose grave threats or otherwise have significant consequences.

From past experience, analysts have found that involving policymakers in the alternative futures exercise is the most effective way to communicate the results of this exploration of alternative outcomes and sensitize them to key uncertainties. Most participants find the process of developing such scenarios as useful as any finished product that attempts to capture the results of the exercise. Analysts and policymakers can benefit from this technique in several ways:

- It provides an effective means of weighing multiple unknown or unknowable factors and presenting a set of plausible outcomes.

- It can help to bound a problem by identifying plausible combinations of uncertain factors.

- It provides a broader analytic framework for calculating the costs, risks, and opportunities presented to policymakers by different outcomes.

❝The future is plural.❞

—Peter Schwartz, author of *The Art of the Long View* and a widely acclaimed scenario developer.

Hypothetical Threats to the Homeland:
Using Spectrums to Define Potential Targets

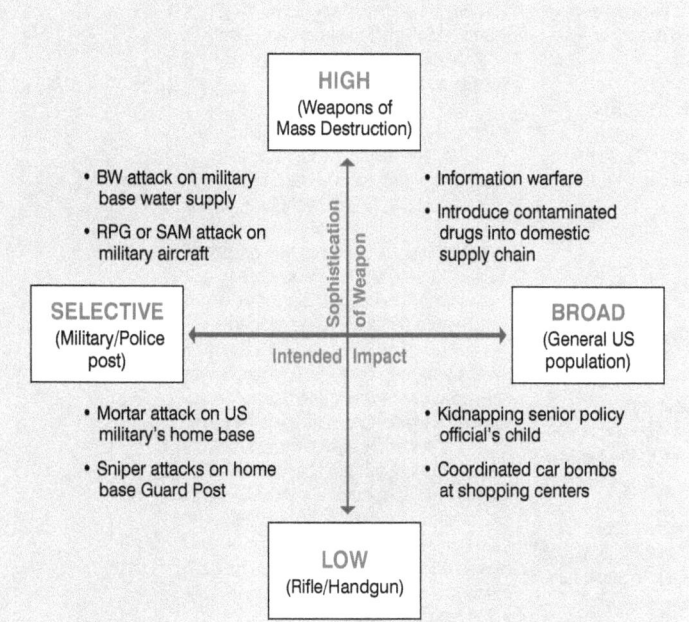

A Futures Exercise. The graphic captures four potential futures to understand how foreign insurgents might carry out an attack on the United States. A brainstorming exercise helped analysts identify two key uncertainties (the sophistication of weapons used by the insurgents and the intended impact of the attack) and arrayed these factors on a graph as the "x" and "y" axes. The four resulting quadrants in the 2 x 2 matrix allowed analysts to visualize potential targets from the various combinations (low to high sophistication of weapons and selective to broad intended impact of an attack). For example, if a group possessed highly sophisticated weapons and intended a broad attack on the United States, potential targets could include computer networks and domestic drug supplies. Having filled in a quadrant, analysts can then turn to devising likely indicators or signposts of such a future.

- It aids analysts and policymakers in anticipating what otherwise would be surprising developments by forcing them to challenge assumptions and consider possible "wild cards" or discontinuous events.

- It generates indicators to monitor for signs that a particular future is becoming more or less likely, so that policies can be reassessed.

THE METHOD

Although there are a variety of ways to develop alternative futures, the most common approach used in both the public and private sectors involves the following steps:

- Develop the "focal issue" by systematically interviewing experts and officials who are examining the general topic.

- Convene a group of experts (both internal and external) to brainstorm about the forces and factors that could affect the focal issue.

- Select by consensus the two most critical and uncertain forces and convert these into axes or continua with the most relevant endpoints assigned.

- Establish the most relevant endpoints for each factor; e.g., if economic growth were the most critical, uncertain force, the endpoints could be "fast" and "slow" or "transformative" and "stabilizing" depending on the type of issue addressed.

- Form a futures matrix by crossing the two chosen axes. The four resulting quadrants provide the basis for characterizing alternative future worlds.

- Generate colorful stories that describe these futures and how they could plausibly come about. Signposts or indicators can then be developed.

Participants, especially policymakers, can then consider how current decisions or strategies would fare in each of the four worlds and identify alternative policies that might work better either across all the futures or in specific ones. By anticipating alternative outcomes, policymakers have a better chance of either devising strategies flexible enough to accommodate multiple outcomes or of being prepared and agile in the face of change.

These structured analytic techniques can be used in a variety of ways when analysts begin a new assessment. Some can be used equally effectively at multiple points in the process and can promote an analyst's ability to keep an open mind, to consider multiple—including highly unlikely—hypotheses, to challenge conventional wisdom, and to assess the impact of important information gaps or deception on analytic judgments and confidence levels. The Timeline for Using Analytic Techniques provides some thoughts on when to use one or more of them during the course of an analyst's research and writing.

Starting Out

At the beginning of an analytic project, analysts are always wise to consider brainstorming and assumptions checks to insure that important factors are not being missed or taken for granted. Similarly, outside-in-thinking can sometimes put an analytic project into a broader international context, in which factors outside the lead analyst's area of responsibility might impact on his or her analytic judgments. For instance, economic assumptions about the price of oil might be key to a regional political analyst's understanding the prospects for political stability in an oil-exporting

A Timeline for Using Analytic Techniques Throughout an Analytic Project

Begin Paper/ Commence Project

Deliver Final Paper/ Brief Key Findings

Brainstorming
Key Assumptions Check
What If? Analysis
High Impact/Low Probability Analysis
Outside-In Thinking

Brainstorming
Key Assumptions Check

Team A/Team B Analysis/Debate

Devil's Advocacy

Red Team

Red Team

Deception Detection   Deception Detection

ACH

Scenarios and Alternative Futures Analysis

Gaming, Modeling, and Simulation*

Indicators

*Gaming, Modeling, and Simulation are among the more sophisticated techniques taught in a more advanced analytic methods course and usually require substantial commitments of analyst time and corporate resources.

country or a underdeveloped country entirely dependent on expensive energy imports. A High Impact/Low Probability assessment can also sensitize analysts early on to the significance of dramatic events that might affect their analytic lines.

Some techniques like Indicators and Signposts or Analysis of Competing Hypotheses (ACH) can be useful throughout a project and revisited periodically as new information is absorbed and analyzed. ACH, in particular, is a good tool to use throughout a project to prevent premature closure and to highlight evidence that is most "discriminating" in making an analytic argument. Alternative Futures analysis is similarly useful at the beginning of a project, but can amount to the structure for the entire project.

Hypothesis Testing

As an analytic project takes shape, and hypotheses are being formed about the key intelligence question, it can be appropriate to use one or another contrarian technique to challenge the conventional analytic line that is being developed. If the assessment contains strong judgments about an adversary's behavior, then challenging this view with a "Red Team" effort might be a good corrective to too much of a rational actor approach. Also, a review of intelligence gaps at this juncture can also help give the analysts a better degree of confidence in the information base and judgments reached in the assessment.

A Final Check

As the assessment is being finalized, it can still be useful to review key assumptions as a sanity check on the underlying logic of the analysis. A brainstorming session also may be helpful to insure that no plausible hypothesis has been dismissed or left unaddressed. If a firm consensus has formed around an analytic line and has not been seriously questioned in some time, then a Devil's Advocacy exercise could be useful. Analysts might also use a final review to decide if they have identified a list of key indicators for future developments. This can be an important guide to include in the assessment as a way to track future developments and monitor whether the analytic judgments reached are being realized or in need of revision.

Graham Allison, *Essence of Decision: Explaining the Cuban Missile Crisis*: Examines the Kennedy Administration's decisionmaking style from alternative perspectives of the "rational actor," "organizational actor," and "bureaucratic politics" models.

Max Bazerman and Michael D. Watkins, *Predictable Surprises: The Disasters You Should Have Seen Coming and How To Prevent Them*. Examines the cognitive, organizational and political causes of some predictable surprises and outlines steps to overcome them.

Richard Betts, *Surprise Attack: Lessons for Defense Planning*. Explains why surprise attacks historically have succeeded and argues that the US needs strategies for avoiding surprise or at least reducing their consequences. Uses examples from World War II, Korea, and the Middle East.

Josh Epstein and Rob Axtell, *Sugarscape: Creating Artificial Societies from the Ground Up*. Develops a very simple agent-based model of a silicon-based society and then does simulations of various social, economic and political phenomena, including conflict.

Malcolm Gladwell, *The Tipping Point: How Little Things Can Make a Big Difference*. Examines how social trends, ideas, and products emerge from nowhere and take hold.

Cynthia M. Grabo, *Anticipating Surprises: Analysis for Strategic Warning*. Examines distinctive ingredients of the analytical method of intelligence and suggests ways of improving warning assessments.

Richards J. Heuer, Jr., *The Psychology of Intelligence Analysis*. Examines the impediments to good analysis and provides techniques for overcoming mind-sets and cognitive biases.

Barry Hughes, *International Futures*. Develops scenarios for international relations using a simulation tool contained in a CD ROM in the back jacket.

Robert Jervis, *Perception and Misperception in International Politics*. Examines how policymakers learn from history, perceive complexity, and form and change their beliefs.

Gary Klein, *Intuition At Work*. Shows how developing one's intuition can improve your analytic skills and that it is a "learnable" technique.

Richard E. Neustadt and Ernest R. May, *Thinking in Time: The Uses of History for Decisionmakers*. Uses case study methods to identify the perils of historical analogies and recommends identifying what is "known, unclear and presumed."

Peter Schwartz, *The Art of the Long View: Planning for the Future in an Uncertain World*. Explains the "scenario" approach pioneered at Royal Dutch Shell and argues for making strategic decisions that will be sound for "all plausible futures."

James Surowiecki, *The Wisdom of Crowds*. Argues that diversity and independence of even non-expert individuals in groups, properly organized, can reach more accurate forecasts than individual experts.

M. Mitchell Waldrop, *Complexity: The Emerging Science at the Edge of Disorder and Chaos*. Introduces the literature of complex systems and suggests why forecasting anything complicated is so difficult.